Property of
HEBRON PUBLIC SCHOOL LIBRARY

DISCARD

W9-AWJ-432

Thomas Alva Edison

THOMAS ALVA EDISON

by Christopher Lampton

Franklin Watts
New York/London/Toronto/Sydney/1988
A First Book

Cover photograph courtesy of General Electric.
Photographs courtesy of: The Bettmann Archive, Inc.: pp. 2, 8, 17, 34, 37,
48 (bottom), 57, 63, 77, 81, 82; The Granger Collection: pp. 11, 21, 31, 86;
General Electric: pp. 14, 42, 48, 72; U.S. Department of the Interior,
National Park Service, Edison National Historic Site: pp. 19, 22, 33, 40,
46, 49, 51, 53, 55, 60, 65, 66, 69, 74 (top), 76, 84, 89; Brown Brothers: pp. 25,
48 (top), 61, 87; UPI/Bettmann Newsphotos: pp. 27, 74 (bottom), 75, 90.

Library of Congress Cataloging-in-Publication Data

Lampton, Christopher.
Thomas Alva Edison

(A First book)
Bibliography: p.
Includes index.
Summary: Traces the life and contributions of the
famous inventor whose inventions such as the electric
light blub and photography helped change the world.
1.   Edison, Thomas A. (Thomas Alva), 1847-1931—
Biography—Juvenile literature.   2.   Inventors—United
States—Biography—Juvenile literature.   [1.   Edison,
Thomas A. (Thomas Alva), 1847-1931.   2.   Inventors]
I. Title
TK140.E3L36   1988   621.3'092'4 [B] [92]   87-25438
ISBN 0-531-10491-5

Copyright © 1988 by Christopher Lampton
All rights reserved
Printed in the United States
5   4   3   2   1

Contents

Thomas Alva Edison

INTRODUCTION

The Man Who Changed the World

The world into which Thomas Alva Edison was born was very different from the one in which he died. It was a world that you might find rather strange, if you were to wake up one morning and find yourself mysteriously transported to 1847. It was a world without radios and televisions, a world where no one had ever heard of the automobile, airplane, or motion picture. It was a world where 10 miles (16 km) was a great distance, where a trip from one side of the United States to the other took many months and was as grueling as a trip to Mars might be today. It was a world in which you would not be able to pick up a phone and call a friend in another state and in which news often took weeks or months to work its way across the nation and around the world.

But the world in which Edison died, eighty-four years later, was very much like the world we know today. Passenger airplanes flew daily across the ocean, automobiles clogged the streets of all but the smallest towns, movies were big business, radios carried news instantly into the most remote corners of the earth, and television was just around the corner.

Edison lived during a period when technology—the tools that we use to make the world a better place—changed and expanded faster than ever before. He lived in the great age of invention, a time when determined and talented individuals built devices that changed the way people looked at the world around them, devices like the telephone, automobile, and radio.

Edison was the greatest of these inventors and was recognized as such in his own lifetime. Even a list of just his most important inventions would be too long to fit on this page, but you are probably already familiar with at least two of them: the phonograph, ancestor of today's stereos and compact disc players, and the electric lightbulb. Edison also made significant contributions to the telegraph, the telephone, the stock ticker, the motion picture . . . and, well, the list goes on and on.

The greatest of Edison's inventions, however, is something that you see every day and probably don't think about. Yet without it the world would be a very different place, much more like the world in which Edison was born than the one in which he died. It is the electric socket on the wall—or, to be more accurate, the system of wires, electric stations, and power generators that bring the electricity to that socket. Without the electricity that flows into that socket we would not have television, radio, refrigerators, washing machines, furnaces, air conditioners, home computers, and any of the host of other appliances that plug into those sockets. Of course, we could run some of those appliances with batteries, but not all of them. It is this electric power supply system that makes electricity available to everyone, all the time, and it is electricity that enables the modern world to function.

Thomas Edison helped bring electricity to the world. If the world changed while Thomas Edison lived, it was at least in part because he helped to change it. Not many people have the chance to change the world as much as Edison did. Edison lived at a time when the world was ready for important technological changes, and he was the perfect man to help bring those changes about. He

Without the electric power industry,
started by Thomas Edison,
we would not have televisions,
radio, refrigerators, and so on.

had a sharp mind, a tremendous amount of energy, and the patience to try over and over again until he could find a way to make an invention work the way he wanted it to. Even without Thomas Edison we might still today have electric sockets in the wall, and there would probably be phonographs and electric lightbulbs. But without Edison those things would have come along later than they did and might not have worked the same way that they do. The world we know today would surely be different if Thomas Edison had never lived.

By the time he was an old man, there were people who believed that Thomas Edison could do anything. That wasn't true, of course, but for a time in the late nineteenth century it looked as though Edison just might be able to perform a miracle or two. . . .

CHAPTER ONE

Birth of a Legend

Thomas Alva Edison was born on February 11, 1847, in the small town of Milan, Ohio. He would have been the youngest of seven children, but three of his brothers and sisters died before he was born. The three that survived were so much older than he was that he might as well have been an only child. His mother, Nancy, lavished on him all the love that she was unable to give her dead children.

By all accounts Al, as young Edison was known, was a happy child, but he was prone to mischief and frequently got into trouble with his parents, especially his father. Much of this mischief arose from the same curiosity that would later make him a great inventor. For instance, when he was only six years old, he set fire to his father's barn. Later, he explained that he just wanted "to see what it would do."[1] As punishment, his father whipped him in the village square, in front of an audience of townspeople.

The boy who would later become the greatest inventor of his time was not a good student. His schoolteacher, the Reverend G.B. Engle, called him "addled." His father agreed, and Al himself was unsure of his own intelligence. "My father thought I was

Nancy Elliott Edison and Edison's father,
Samuel, in his later years
Below: Edison's birthplace in Milan, Ohio

stupid, and I almost decided I must be a dunce," he said many years later.[2] We now know that Al wasn't really stupid. Probably, he was too bright. He had a restless mind and did not want to concentrate on lessons designed for slower students.

To make matters worse, Edison contracted scarlet fever at the age of seven, and the disease affected his hearing. For the rest of his life he had trouble hearing, and by old age he was almost completely deaf.

Recognizing that her son needed a special education, Al's mother took him out of school at the age of seven and began to teach him herself. She thought highly of Al's ability to learn and surrounded him with books that would have been difficult for the average elementary school student, then or now, books such as *The Decline and Fall of the Roman Empire* and David Hume's *History of England*, as well as works by William Shakespeare and Charles Dickens. Far from being frightened or bored by these books, Al read them avidly and found other books to read on his own. Edison probably learned as much from these books as he learned from the lessons his mother taught him.

The book that inspired the young Edison more than any other was *The School of Natural Philosophy* by R.G. Parker. It was a book of scientific experiments that a youngster like Edison could conduct at home. Edison soon began collecting chemicals and scientific implements, stowing them in his room so that he could perform Parker's experiments and others of his own devising. His mother, encouraged by her son's enthusiasm, bought him more science books. Soon, he had turned his bedroom into a laboratory, but his mother forced him to move the foul-smelling chemicals to the basement, where he continued with his experiments.

Not all of Al's experiments were very scientific. Once, he experimented with static electricity by wiring together the tails of two cats and rubbing their fur! The result? The cats got mad, Edison got scratched, and the cause of science was not much advanced.

[15]

As this "experiment" illustrates, Edison was fascinated by electricity. And the electrical device that fascinated him most was the telegraph.

The telegraph was one of the greatest inventions of the mid-nineteenth century, though it has almost been forgotten today. It is the ancestor of the communications devices that are now so common, for example, the telephone, radio, television, and computer modem. Invented in 1838 by Samuel F. B. Morse, the telegraph was a device used for transmitting messages over long distances by wire. A telegraph operator would translate the message into Morse code, a series of "dots" and "dashes" (clicking sounds that represented the letters of the alphabet), and tap out the message on a telegraph "key." The message would be carried electrically to another city, where a second operator would translate the message back into English and write it down on paper. The telegraph greatly increased the speed at which news and important information could travel across the country.

Thomas Edison, the boy experimenter, built his own telegraphs so that he could send messages to friends the way that a young person today might talk to friends on the telephone. These telegraphs were crude, but they worked, and they were not the last telegraphs that Thomas Edison would build. In fact, it would be the telegraph that would later launch Edison's career as the greatest inventor of his time.

As he became better educated and more ambitious, the young Edison's experiments became more and more expensive to finance. Unfortunately, his once well-to-do family had by then fallen on hard times, and Edison was forced to go to work, both to

Samuel F. B. Morse
(1791–1872)

support his experiments and to help his family. So it was that at the age of twelve, Al Edison went to work on the railroad.

———

In the middle of the nineteenth century a network of railroads was being built across the United States. By 1859 the railroad had come to Port Huron, Michigan, the town to which the Edisons had moved when Al was seven years old. With the help of his father, young Al secured a job with the railroad selling newspapers on the "mixed train" to Detroit, so-called because it carried both passengers and freight.

The train left Port Huron at 7 A.M., so Al had to leave for work each morning before dawn. The train returned to Port Huron at 9:30 in the evening. Needless to say, Al didn't spend much time at home, and when he did, he didn't sleep much. He spent his nights talking to a neighbor on his homemade telegraph, practicing the Morse code.

Actually, he didn't mind the long working hours. By some accounts, he was having the time of his life. When he wasn't busy with his job of selling newspapers, magazines, and candies, he would spend his time on the train reading, or thinking about experiments that he wanted to perform. Within a year, he had persuaded the trainman for whom he was working to let him build a laboratory on the train so that he could perform experiments in the baggage car. However, when Edison was about fifteen years old, one of these experiments ended disastrously. Some of his chemicals spilled, and the baggage car caught fire. The trainman tossed Edison's laboratory off the train.

*Al at age
fourteen*

Although Edison had been partially deaf since his bout with scarlet fever years earlier, he was able to function well despite his handicap. He claimed later that he was able to hear ordinary conversation on board the train because people were forced to shout to be heard over the noise of the train itself, which he barely heard.

Young Edison was a hard worker. He knew the value of money, and he never missed a chance to earn some. One of his cleverest money-making schemes was devised on the spur of the moment, during the American Civil War, when he heard that a major battle had taken place at Shiloh.

As a newspaper boy, Al had the opportunity to make friends with the publishers of the *Detroit Free Press*. Often he would stop by their offices to find out what the day's headlines would be, so that he could decide how many copies he was likely to sell. When he heard about the Battle of Shiloh, he knew the day's paper would be a hot item. He laid in a large supply and arranged to have word of the battle telegraphed ahead to the next station. Edison later told the story this way:

When I got to the first station on the run . . . the platform was crowded with men and women. After one look at the crowd I raised the price to ten cents. I sold thirty-five papers. At Mount Clemens, where I usually sold six papers, the crowd was there too . . . I raised the price from ten cents to fifteen. . . . It had been my practice at Port Huron to jump from the train at about one quarter of a mile from the station where the train generally slackened speed. I had drawn several loads of sand to this point and had become quite expert. The little Dutch boy with the horse usually met me there. When the wagon approached the outskirts of town I was met by a large crowd. I then yelled: "Twenty-five cents, gentlemen. I haven't enough to go around!"[3]

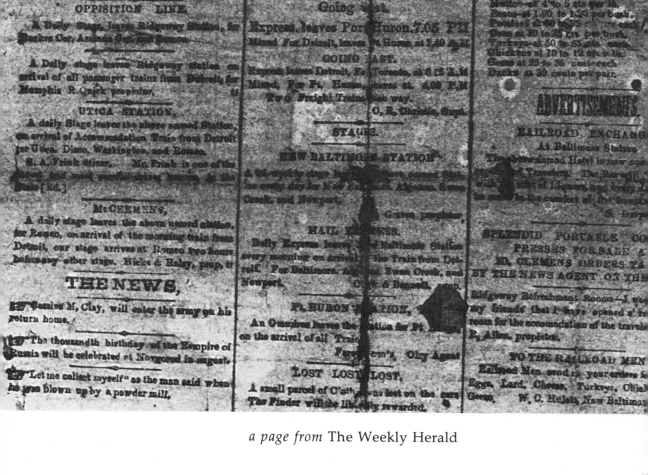

a page from The Weekly Herald

Obviously, there was money in newspapers, so the enterprising young Edison decided to found his own. In 1862, he began publishing *The Weekly Herald*, a small newspaper that he wrote, printed, and sold on trains from Port Huron to Detroit at a grand price of 8¢ a copy, remarkably expensive for those days.

But Edison wanted to be more than just a newspaper boy. One of his early dreams was to be a railroad engineer, an occupation every bit as exciting in the 1860s as piloting a jet plane is now. He got his chance in 1862 when the engineer of the Detroit mixed train allowed him to take the wheel. Young Al piloted the train while the engineer and his fireman—the railroad equivalent of a co-pilot—snoozed the afternoon away. Soon Edison noticed that the smoke rising out of the engine's smokestack was unusually black; although he didn't realize it, the black "smoke" was actually mud formed by his pumping too much water into the engine. When he stopped the train to look for the cause of the problem, both he and the train ended up coated with the thick, black mud. This was the last time Edison would try his hand at being a railroad engineer.

His real ambition, though, was to become a telegraph operator. It was the railroad, ironically, that helped him realize it. One day, while waiting on a station platform, Edison saw a boxcar rolling down the track toward a young boy. He rescued the boy before the car could roll over him. The boy's father, stationmaster J.U. Mackenzie, gratefully repaid Edison by tutoring him in telegraph operations. By the end of 1862, the sixteen-year-old Thomas Edison was ready to set out on a new career, as a "plug" telegrapher.

CHAPTER TWO

Traveling Telegrapher

If you have ever used a typewriter or the keyboard of a computer, or even watched someone else use these things, you have some idea of what a telegrapher of the 1860s did.

Like typists—that is, people who type on keyboards—the telegraphers sat at desks and typed on "keys." The difference was that the telegrapher had only a single key on which to type, while a typist today has an entire keyboard full. Instead of typing on keys marked with letters of the alphabet, the telegrapher typed dots and dashes—short and long taps on the keys—which represented letters of the alphabet, according to the Morse code.

Also like typists, telegraphers were judged by the speed at which they could type messages. A fast telegrapher could send a message at forty-five words per minute, or more. A slow or inexperienced telegrapher would send messages at a slower speed. Slow telegraphers were called "plug" telegraphers, because they "just plugged along."

When he started his career in telegraphy, Edison was a plug telegrapher. Fortunately, there were a lot of jobs available even for slow telegraphers, and so Edison had no trouble finding work.

an early telegraph instrument

But, as ever, young Al seemed to have a knack for getting into trouble.

One of his first jobs, in 1864, was as a railroad dispatcher at Stratford Junction in Ontario, Canada, not far from Port Huron. Edison worked the night shift, from seven in the evening to seven in the morning, sending and receiving telegraph messages and signaling trains to let them know when it was safe to pass the station.

The job was easy enough, so easy that Edison took to spending his working hours reading, performing experiments, or catching up on sleep. Every few hours, however, Edison was expected to send a signal to the head office to let them know he was still on the job. How could he snooze and still send this signal? The ingenious Edison rigged up a clockwork mechanism to send the signal automatically at the expected times.

One night, however, Edison neglected to signal a passing train to let it know that another train, heading in the opposite direction, was using the same track. Terrified that his mistake would lead to a head-on collision between the two trains, Edison rushed belatedly into the night and tried to catch up with the train on foot. "The night was dark," Edison wrote later, "and I fell into a culvert and was knocked senseless."[4]

The trains did not collide, but Edison was called up before the general manager of the railroad to explain his offense. Afraid that he might end up in jail, Edison slipped away while the general manager was distracted by visitors, caught a train, and fled Canada for the United States.

His next job was in Adrian, Michigan, but after only a short time he was fired. He did little better at his next job, in Fort

Edison at age twenty

Wayne. In fact, he was hired and fired from four jobs in 1864 alone.

In part, his poor job record was a result of his inattentiveness and a tendency to daydream about things that interested him more than his work. Sometimes Edison would stop in the middle of receiving a telegraph message, tell the operator at the other end to wait, and jot down some notes about an invention he was working on.

But some of his problems may also have been due in part to his personality. He was a loner who generally didn't get along well with his co-workers or his supervisors. He dressed eccentrically, didn't pay much attention to his appearance, and may well have come across as more than a little arrogant. In telegraphy circles, Edison's nickname was "The Looney."

Edison also had a penchant for practical jokes, which he frequently combined with his love of invention and experimentation. At one job he wired up an electrical generator and connected it to a trough of water where workers washed up on the job. As each worker arrived at the trough and plunged his hands into the water, he received a jolt of electricity. Certainly, some of the workers must have been less than amused by this stunt, but as each worker realized how he had been tricked, he joined the crowd of workers waiting on the sidelines to see the *next* worker get jolted.

At one office, the old-time telegraphers decided to play a joke on Edison, but he cleverly turned the tables on them. To test the newly arrived Edison's skill at receiving messages, they arranged for an experienced telegrapher in New York to send messages at a speed too fast for Edison to write them down. But by this time the plug telegrapher had honed his skills in receiving messages, and he had no trouble keeping up as the New York operator transmitted faster and faster. Finally, as the other telegraphers watched, Edison sent a message back to the New York operator: "Say, young man, change off and send with your other foot!"[5]

By the end of 1864, Edison was working for Western Union, a

[28]

company that would play an important role in his future career as an inventor. In the beginning, he was still just a plug telegrapher, drifting from one Western Union office to another. But by 1865 he had gained his first-class operator's license. In truth, Edison had not only learned to send messages at speeds greater than forty-five words per minute, but he had become one of the fastest message receivers in the telegraph business. Not only could he take down incoming messages at breakneck speed, but he could do so in very neat handwriting, a prized skill.

It was while working as a telegrapher that Edison finally produced some practical inventions. One, from his early days in the business, was a device that slowed down incoming telegraph messages by punching the messages on a long roll of paper and "playing them back" on a second telegraph at a different speed. This allowed the young telegrapher to take down the messages at his own speed.

But it was not Edison's fate to remain a telegrapher forever. He was cut out for other things. His time at the telegraph key was not wasted, however. Telegraphy provided an education for young Al. As he tapped out important news stories he learned about the world around him, and that information would hold him in good stead in the years to come. For a time, Edison even considered becoming a reporter. Finally, he learned how telegraphs and other electrical devices worked. Soon, he would become one of the world's greatest experts on this subject.

By late 1867, Edison's career as a telegrapher was nearly over. He had lost too many jobs; he was running out of places to go. In despair, he returned to his parents' home, sad and broke. But things at home were not going well. His parents had been forced to sell their house and move elsewhere. His mother was ill and increasingly depressed and his father was rarely home.

Young Thomas Edison chose not to stay there. Shortly after arriving he left again for Boston to make one last try at telegraphy. But he didn't stick with it. Within a year he had found a new line of work: inventor.

[29]

CHAPTER THREE

Gold Tickers and the
Duplex Telegraph

In 1869 Edison announced, in a telegraph trade journal, that he would "hereafter devote his full time to bringing out his inventions." What had inspired this change of professions?

While working as a telegraph operator, Edison had become aware of an important problem that needed to be solved: how to send two messages at the same time on a single telegraph wire.

Why send two messages over the same wire? In the 1860s, the telegraph was the only means of long-distance communication. There were no telephones or radios, and there were only a limited number of telegraph wires. Those wires crackled with all the messages that they could handle, and a lot of people who wanted to send messages by telegraph were turned away, especially during the "peak" hours of the day, when the largest number of messages were being sent. If it were possible to send two messages on the same wire, one traveling in one direction and the other traveling in the other direction, twice as many messages could be sent—and the telegraph companies would make twice as much money. So a lot of inventors, including Thomas Edison, were trying to invent a "duplex" telegraph.

Telegraph offices, such as this one run by the American Telegraph Company in New York, bustled with activity in the mid-nineteenth century.

Edison built his first duplex telegraph while he was still a telegraph operator, but it didn't work as well as it might have. For one thing, he didn't have enough money to properly carry out his experiments. But while working in Boston, he met an important businessman who loaned him the money to start him on the road to becoming a successful inventor.

Although Edison was supposed to use this money to build a duplex telegraph, his roving mind immediately turned to the possibility of other inventions. One was an automatic voting machine to be used by Congress, so that senators and representatives could vote by pressing buttons rather than by shouting out a long series of ayes and nays. The device worked quite well, but Congress wasn't the least bit interested in it; the senators and representatives preferred their old way of voting.

Edison wasn't discouraged. His next invention was an automatic gold ticker, a device that could be installed in the offices of well-to-do businesspeople who needed to know the current price of gold to help them make decisions about their investments. Information about current gold prices would be sent through long wires from the Boston Gold Exchange, where gold was sold and bought, to the machines themselves, just as messages were carried from telegraph to telegraph. Edison rented thirty of these tickers to businesses, stringing the wires from the Gold Exchange across the rooftops of Boston.

Even while working on these inventions, Edison did not forget about the duplex telegraph. In fact, he built one duplex after another, each one better than its predecessor but still not good enough to be used by the major telegraph companies. His experiments with the duplex used up a lot of money, and Edison soon found himself in debt. Eventually, he was completely penniless. He decided at this point that perhaps Boston was not the town in which to make his fortune, and so he pulled up stakes and moved to New York City.

Edison's automatic voting machine

*young Edison at work on
an improved telegraph system*

Edison arrived in New York without a single possession other than the clothes on his back. He didn't even have a place to stay. He hoped to find an old friend who could lend him money and give him a floor to sleep on, but the only friend he found was just as broke as he was and could only lend him a dollar. Undaunted, Edison went to the offices of Franklin L. Pope, an electrical engineer with the Gold Indicator Company, which rented gold tickers similar to those Edison had rented in Boston. Pope was impressed with Edison. He was unable to offer him a job, but he did give him a place to sleep and to perform his experiments: the basement of one of the company's offices.

For weeks Edison lived on a small cot at the Gold Indicator Company, surviving on a diet of apple dumplings and coffee. (He enjoyed this diet so much that he continued to live on it even after he had the money to purchase better food.) And then he was presented with what can only be called a "golden opportunity."

You may have wondered why knowing the price of gold was so important to businesses that they would pay to have machines installed in their offices to inform them of the current price. In the 1860s, the price of gold was constantly changing. People known as speculators made a living out of buying and selling gold. The price of gold was determined by how much speculators were willing to pay for it. A speculator made money by buying gold, then finding another speculator who would buy it for a higher price. Then the second speculator would find a third speculator who would pay an even higher price for it. This was how speculators made money and why the price of gold kept changing.

The buying and selling of gold took place at the Gold Exchange. (In New York, as opposed to Boston, the Gold Exchange was actually part of the Stock Exchange, which controlled the buying and selling of many things besides gold.) As the price of gold changed, the Gold Indicator Company sent the changing price by wire to little machines owned by speculators all over New York. Tiny wheels with numbers painted on them rotated inside these machines, turning in one direction if the price went up and in the other direction if the price went down. Speculators watched these changing numbers. When the price of gold was high, they sold it and made a profit. When the price of gold was low, they bought it with the hope that it would go back up again, which it usually did.

One day in 1869, the master machine in the Gold Indicator Company office broke down. All of the machines in the offices of speculators stopped. Frantic to know the current price of gold, the speculators sent messengers to the Gold Indicator office. Three hundred messengers arrived at the office almost simultaneously. Dr. Samuel S. Laws, who ran the Gold Indicator Company, panicked. When Edison suggested that he might be able to repair the gold ticker, Laws yelled, "Fix it! Fix it! Be quick, for God's sake!"[6]

Edison was quick enough. Within two hours, he had fished a broken spring out of the mechanism and gotten the machine running once more, saving the day. Laws, impressed by the young man's ingenuity, offered Edison a job with the company.

Edison accepted. Over the next few months he worked with Laws to develop an improved ticker. By July of 1869, when Franklin Pope resigned to go into business for himself, Edison took over Pope's position as chief engineer.

The gold ticker that Edison developed for Laws was so successful that it caught the attention of Western Union, which ran a rival gold price service. In fact, Western Union was so impressed by the machine that they bought the Gold Indicator Company.

Edison's career as a professional inventor was well underway. In October of 1869 he started his own company, in partnership with Pope and another man. He lived at Pope's home in Elizabeth, New Jersey, and worked at a machine shop in Jersey City. The new company, which was called Pope, Edison and Company, took out patents on seven new telegraphs and at least one new gold ticker.

Edison's improved stock ticker machine

When Pope, Edison and Company offered its own gold price service based around this new ticker, Western Union once again became interested and bought out the company, just as it had earlier bought out the Gold Indicator Company. Edison, however, was angered that most of the money went to his two partners, even though he felt he was the one who had done most of the work. He broke up the partnership and went to work for himself.

But his hard work with Pope, Edison and Company did not go unnoticed. General Marshall Lefferts, formerly of the Gold Indicator Company and now an employee of Western Union, offered Edison a job developing stock tickers (which were similar to gold tickers) for Western Union. Edison was somewhat reluctant to go back to work for his old employer, but he knew better than to turn down money that could be used for financing new inventions.

Edison lived up to Lefferts' expectations. When he developed an improved stock ticker, Lefferts asked him how much he wanted for the invention. Edison, who was still somewhat uncertain as a businessman, asked Lefferts to make him an offer, figuring that he would get perhaps $5,000 for his work. Lefferts offered him $40,000. Edison nearly fainted. He accepted the offer and Marshall started to write him a check for the amount. So unaccustomed was Edison to having such large sums of money that he didn't even know how to deposit the check in a bank and had to ask Lefferts to give him the money in cash instead.

Or, at least, this was how Edison told the story many years later. Since Edison soon proved to be very canny at making money (if not always at keeping it), the story may be more than a little exaggerated. Edison may have guessed that Lefferts would offer him more money if he kept his mouth shut, and he may have felt that cash was safer than checks.

If so, the ploy worked. For the first time in his life, Edison had a large sum of money . . . and he had no problem figuring out what to do with it.

CHAPTER FOUR

Thomas Edison, Businessman

Edison used the money he had received from Lefferts to set up a new company in Newark, New Jersey. This company, called Edison & Unger, manufactured stock tickers for Western Union. (William Unger, Edison's partner in the new company, was an employee of Marshall Lefferts.) To build the stock tickers, Edison hired fifty workers, over whom he served as a foreman. He wrote his parents a letter about his new company, joking that "I am now what 'you' Democrats call 'a Bloated Eastern Manufacturer.' "[7]

Among the workers hired by this "Bloated Eastern Manufacturer" were John Ott, a young machinist with whom Edison had worked in Jersey City; Charles Batchelor, an English machinist and draftsman; John Kruesi, a former clockmaker from Switzerland; and Sigmund Bergmann, a German mechanic. These were men who would remain with Edison for many years.

All of those, in fact, who worked for Edison liked the young inventor very much. He was not an aloof and distant boss. He was one of them. He was unafraid to get his hands dirty, to work on the machines along with the rest of them. He joked with them, encouraged them to do their best work, and understood their

*the offices of Edison & Unger
in Newark, New Jersey*

problems. Edison, after all, loved his work. He put in as many hours in the shop as even the most dedicated of his employees, and he sometimes slept in the shop overnight, when a particularly difficult job needed to be finished.

Alas, while Edison may have been an excellent boss, he was poor at bookkeeping and never remembered to pay bills until his creditors threatened to sue. He frequently invested more money than he could afford in the purchase of new equipment. Later, Edison would hire clerks to take care of the bookkeeping for him, but money worries would pursue him throughout his career. He would earn millions of dollars, but he would often spend it as quickly as he would get it.

In 1871, Edison was approached by an organization called the Automatic Telegraph Company, which owned the patent rights to a new type of telegraph invented by George D. Little. This new telegraph, which transmitted messages that had been punched onto a roll of paper, needed some improvements before it could be put to use. The Automatic Telegraph Company asked Edison to make those improvements. With the money he received for this, Edison founded yet another company, Edison & Murray, in partnership with Joseph T. Murray. The new company was also based in Newark, just down the road from Edison & Unger.

Ironically, the Automatic Telegraph Company was a rival of Western Union, for whom Edison was already working. This didn't seem to bother Edison, who just wanted the chance to apply his ingenuity to the job of inventing. After all, he was building stock tickers for Western Union and telegraphs for the Automatic Telegraph Company.

In 1871, employees in Edison's laboratory noticed that he had begun paying particular attention to one of his employees, a Miss Mary Stilwell. The usually hard-working Edison seemed to be finding every excuse to spend time in Miss Stilwell's presence, and it soon became obvious that he had fallen in love. Apparently Miss Stilwell reciprocated his feelings, because by Christmas they were married. Mary Stilwell became Mary Edison.

[41]

Marriage, however, did little to change Edison's work habits. He still spent most of his time in the shop. His wife, who had quit her job in the shop after the wedding, would go for days without seeing her husband. Edison loved her, but he also loved his work. Legend has it that he spent the evening of his wedding day hard at work in the laboratory and had to be reminded that he had just gotten married and that his new wife would be expecting him at home. This probably isn't true. Nonetheless, Edison's work may have taken precedence over his marriage. In fact, when the couple had their first two children, a girl and a boy, they were nicknamed Dot and Dash, in honor of Edison's work on the telegraph.

———

In April of 1873, the Automatic Telegraph Company sent Edison to Europe to negotiate the sale of one of his inventions. When he returned, he found his Newark shops on the verge of being closed down to pay off his debts. His wife had borrowed enough money to save the day, but Edison had to put in many months of hard work to raise new cash. He was forced to rearrange his businesses. Edison & Unger was sold. He opened a new shop in partnership with George Harrington, a former assistant secretary of the U.S. Treasury, but that, too, was sold shortly thereafter.

Edison was certain now that his fortune lay in the "diplex" telegraph, a variation on the duplex. The duplex telegraph could send two messages in opposite directions; the diplex, as Edison saw it, would send two messages in the *same* direction. And, if a diplex was possible, then what was to stop Edison from building a "quadruplex," which could send *four* messages at one time, two in each direction?

Mary Stilwell Edison,
at sixteen

By 1874, Edison had built a working quadruplex, for Western Union. But Western Union was slow to pay him for it and he needed the money desperately to pay off his debts. In anger, Edison stormed away from Western Union and went into the employ of their rival, the Atlantic & Pacific Telegraph Company, which owned the Automatic Telegraph Company.

A major "telegraphic war" ensued between the two giant companies, in which Edison's inventions were a major weapon. The battle finally ended up in court, where the two companies fought over the patent rights to Edison's ingenious new telegraphs.

Edison, however, had little interest in this war. He just wanted to continue working on his inventions, and he was willing to do his work for whatever company would pay him the most for it. He was a member of a new breed, a free-lance inventor who sold his new inventions to the highest bidder. He was already developing a reputation as one of the best of this breed. As the market for his inventions grew, Edison found himself outgrowing the laboratories that he had founded in Newark. It was time to build a new laboratory, an invention factory, where he could pursue all of the new ideas that flickered through his brilliant mind. And so it was that Edison moved to Menlo Park, New Jersey.

CHAPTER FIVE

The Invention Factory

There had never been anything quite like it before. From the outside, it looked like an ordinary white farmhouse, 100 feet (30 m) long and 30 feet (9 m) wide, with a few outbuildings and a picket fence around it. But inside was the world's first invention factory, a laboratory designed specifically for the purpose of inventing new devices.

Today, invention factories are common, but they are usually run by large corporations such as Dupont or AT&T. In 1876, no one had heard of such a thing. In fact, some historians believe that this invention factory was itself Edison's greatest invention.

In his laboratory at Menlo Park, Edison could get away from the hectic world of the city and do what he did best: build new things. Naturally, some of the things that he built were new models of the telegraph, but now another invention had seized his imagination: the telephone.

As everyone knows, the telephone was invented by Alexander Graham Bell, another great nineteenth-century inventor. It was a kind of "speaking telegraph." Instead of transmitting dots and dashes along a wire, the telephone transmitted sounds, so that a

winter at Edison's Menlo Park Laboratory,
as depicted by R. F. Outcault

person holding a telephone at one end of a wire could hear the voice of a person speaking into a telephone at the other end. This seems quite commonplace today, of course, when telephones can be found in every home and office. But in the 1870s it was an amazing invention, destined to revolutionize the way people communicated with one another.

The telephone is actually two inventions, a transmitter that converts sound into electricity and a receiver that converts the electricity back into sound. When you speak into a telephone, you are speaking into the transmitter; when you listen to the telephone, you are listening to the receiver.

In Bell's telephone, however, the transmitter and receiver were one device. This created two problems. One was that the person using the phone had to move it rapidly from mouth to ear in order to carry on a conversation. The other was that, while Bell's telephone made a pretty good receiver, it was a poor transmitter. A person attempting to talk to another person over Bell's invention was forced to shout loudly in order to be heard.

At one time, Edison had attempted to develop his own "speaking telegraph." When it became obvious that Bell's invention offered more room for improvement, Edison began working on it, producing a transmitter that was far superior to Bell's. The Bell telephone could carry audible messages only a few miles, while the Edison telephone worked over much greater distances. Ultimately, his telephone transmitter made Thomas Edison nearly a quarter of a million dollars and greatly enhanced his reputation.

But while working on the telephone transmitter, Edison's mind turned to a far more ingenious invention, one that no other inventor had even thought of, so far as we know. If it was possible to transmit the human voice electrically, Edison wondered, perhaps it was also possible to *record* the human voice—or any other sound.

Thus, Thomas Edison turned to the invention of the phonograph.

[47]

Alexander Graham Bell
(1847–1922)

the first telephone

*a replica of the tele-
phone developed by Edison*

EDISON'S INVENTIONS

In his long and illustrious career, Edison was issued 1,093 patents, more than any other inventor in history. Below is a list of some of his major inventions, adapted from information in the book *A Streak of Luck* by Robert Conot (see the Recommended Reading section of this book):

telegraph repeater
printer, for stock ticker and telegraph
perforator, for automatic telegraph
mimeograph
electric pen
loudspeaking telephone
phonograph
carbon-button telephone transmitter
tasimeter
incandescent lamp
electric generator
electric locomotive
ore separator
cement works
electric distributing system
kinetoscope (motion picture camera)
microphone
alkaline storage battery

Edison's electric locomotive,
built by him at Menlo Park in 1880

As with the telephone, we tend to take the phonograph for granted today. But one hundred years ago the idea of recording the human voice seemed nothing short of miraculous. And yet Edison's phonograph was actually quite a simple invention—simple but brilliant.

Both the telephone and phonograph are based on a simple principle. When we speak, we create vibrations in the air. When these vibrations enter our ears, they cause our eardrums to vibrate, and our brains interpret these vibrations of the eardrum as sound.

The telephone transmitter converts vibrations in the air into a rising and falling electrical current. The receiver converts the electrical current back into vibrations in the air. It might seem a little silly to go to all this much trouble to convert sound into electricity just to convert it back into sound again. The advantage is that electricity can be carried long distances over wires; hence, the telephone can carry sound over long distances.

It occurred to Edison as he worked on his telephone that if sound could be converted into electricity, it might also be possible to convert it into a form that could be preserved and played back later. To test this theory, he made a sketch of a device consisting of a diaphragm (a thin membrane that would vibrate when struck by sound waves), a needle (attached to the diaphragm), and a rotating cylinder, covered with tinfoil and turned by a handcrank. Making drawings was Edison's favorite way of developing inventions. He possessed a very visual imagination. That is, he saw new ideas and new devices as "pictures" inside his head and then drew those pictures on paper as best he could.

the first known notations
on the phonograph, or
Edison's "speaking telegraph"

Spkg Telegraph

July 18 1877
Chas Batchelor
James Adams

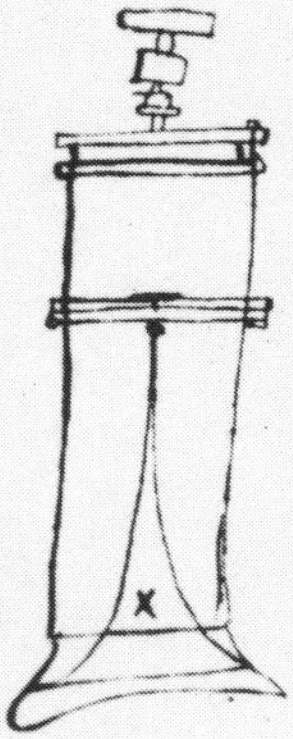

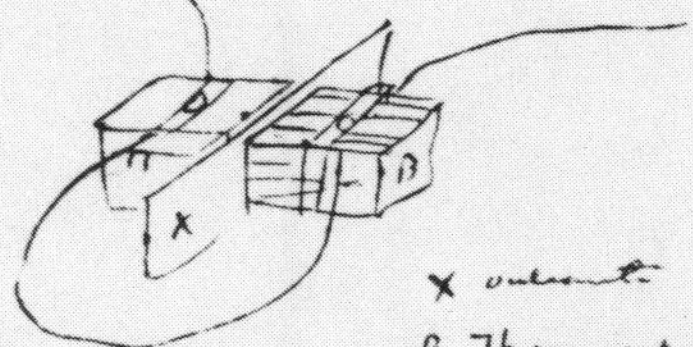

X rubber
B Thermo pile.

X is a rubber membran connected to the
central diaphram and the edges
being near or between the lips in
the act of spkg it gets a vibration
which is communicated to the central
diaphram & thrown in its turn
set the outer diaphragm
vibrating hence the heavier
consonants are reinforced &
made to set the diaphram
in motion we just tried
an experiment similar to
this thus

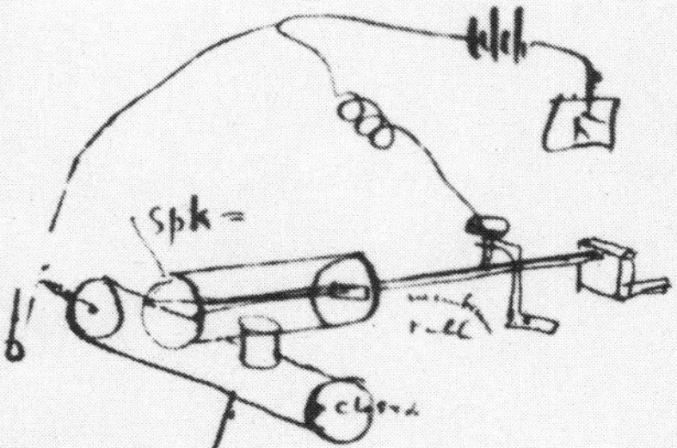

The whole fair
on hissing but
stopped the regular
vowell sounds in
lower tube —

just tried experiment with a diaphram
having an embossing point & held against
paraffin paper moving rapidly the
Spkg vibrations are indented nicely
& there is no doubt that I shall be able to
store up & reproduce automatically at any
future time the human voice perfectly

However, he rarely built the devices himself. Instead, he gave the sketches to his workmen, particularly John Kruesi, who could build them according to Edison's specifications. And, in the case of this new idea of Edison's, it was Kruesi who had the privilege of turning the sketch into the reality.

When it was complete, Edison placed the newly constructed device on a table, turned the crank, and shouted at the diaphragm. What he shouted were the words to a familiar nursery rhyme:

> *Mary had a little lamb,*
> *Its fleece was white as snow,*
> *And everywhere that Mary went*
> *The lamb was sure to go.*

As he spoke, the needle cut a groove into the tinfoil on the cylinder. When he had finished, he placed the needle back on the start of the groove and turned the cylinder again. From the diaphragm came the distinct sound of Edison's voice reciting the words to "Mary Had a Little Lamb."

Edison said later, "I was never so taken aback in all my life. Everybody was astonished. I was always afraid of things that worked the first time."

Kruesi, who had never quite believed that such a remarkable device would work, was equally astonished, or perhaps a little more so. Reportedly, he turned pale and muttered an astonished prayer in German. Perhaps Kruesi was also taken aback because he had bet Edison $2 that the experiment would fail—and he had just lost the bet.

The device, of course, was the phonograph. How did it work? When sound vibrations, such as those created by Edison's voice, struck the diaphragm, it vibrated, and this in turn made the needle vibrate. The groove cut into the tinfoil by the needle recorded these vibrations, and when the needle was run through the groove a second time, the varying depths within the groove forced

[54]

*the original phonograph
patented by Edison in 1878*

the needle to vibrate exactly as it had while making the recording. This, in turn, caused the diaphragm to vibrate, which created sound vibrations in the air very much like those that were in the air when the recording was made, or at least similar enough to fool the ears of those listening to the vibrations.

The phonograph made Edison a celebrity. It was reported widely, in popular magazines and newspapers, and it caught the imagination of both the public and the press. Crowds of reporters showed up at the Menlo Park laboratories to hear demonstrations of this remarkable gadget, and Edison happily obliged them. At one such demonstration, Edison recorded the cornet playing of a Mr. Jules Levy. According to the newspaper account,

Mr. Edison showed the effect of turning the cylinder at different degrees of speed, and then the phonograph proceeded utterly to rout Mr. Levy by playing his tunes in pitches and octaves of astonishing variety. It was interesting to observe the total indifference of the phonograph to the pitch of the note it began upon with regard to the pitch of the note with which it was to end. Gravely singing the tune correctly for half a dozen notes, it would suddenly soar into regions too painfully high for the cornet even by any chance to follow it. Then it delivered the variations on "Yankee Doodle" with a celerity no human fingering of the cornet could rival. . . . The phonograph was equal to any attempts to take unfair advantage of it, and it repeated its songs, and whistles, and speeches, with the cornet music heard so clearly over all, that its victory was unanimously conceded, and amid hilarious crowing from the triumphant cylinder the cornet was ignominiously shut up in its box.[9]

A prima donna warbles a scene from an opera into the phonograph.

[56]

Edison, who thoroughly enjoyed these demonstrations, was even called upon to demonstrate the phonograph at the White House, in front of President Rutherford B. Hayes. To the public at large, Edison became known as the Wizard of Menlo Park, and his laboratories there became a popular tourist attraction.

And yet, despite the unanimous public acclaim that greeted the phonograph, Edison put aside the device for many years and made only a limited attempt to perfect it so that it could be sold commercially. It was almost as though he considered the phonograph a mere toy, with no serious application. And, in fact, the original Edison phonograph was a highly limited device, without the versatility and sound quality of the stereos and compact disc players of today.

But Edison was also tired. He was a hard worker who almost never gave himself a vacation, and in 1878 he may have been too exhausted to go on. Along with a group of scientists from the University of Pennsylvania, he allowed himself to take a trip to the West, though even this "vacation" turned into an occasion for work and experimentation. Edison brought along one of his minor inventions, a device called the tasimeter, which he used to measure small amounts of heat. During an eclipse of the sun he attempted to use the tasimeter to measure the changes in heat that resulted when the moon passed between the earth and the sun. As it turned out, the tasimeter was *too* sensitive and was overwhelmed by the heat of even the eclipsed sun.

But Edison's lively mind must also have been distracted by the prospect of another invention, one that he honestly believed would drastically change the lives of people around the world. That invention, one of Edison's greatest, was the electric lightbulb.

CHAPTER SIX

Let There Be Light

What was so special about the lightbulb? Why did it take a genius the caliber of Thomas Edison to invent it?

Like the phonograph, the incandescent lamp—what we now call the electric lightbulb—is a very simple device. It consists of a thin strand, or filament, of material that glows when electricity is pumped through it. But finding a material that would glow without burning up wasn't easy. Many inventors had tried, and all had failed.

Electric lighting was nothing new. The arc lamp, which produced light by jumping a bright arc of electricity between two electrically charged rods, had been around for decades. But the arc lamp was too bright to be used in homes and offices—and too expensive. Edison saw the lightbulb as an inexpensive device that could illuminate a small room as easily as an auditorium, a device that the average person could afford to buy several of.

How did people illuminate their homes before the lightbulb? Mostly by candlelight, though people who lived in big cities used gaslight. The natural gas used to support the flame of a gaslight was carried from house to house in pipes, much the way electric-

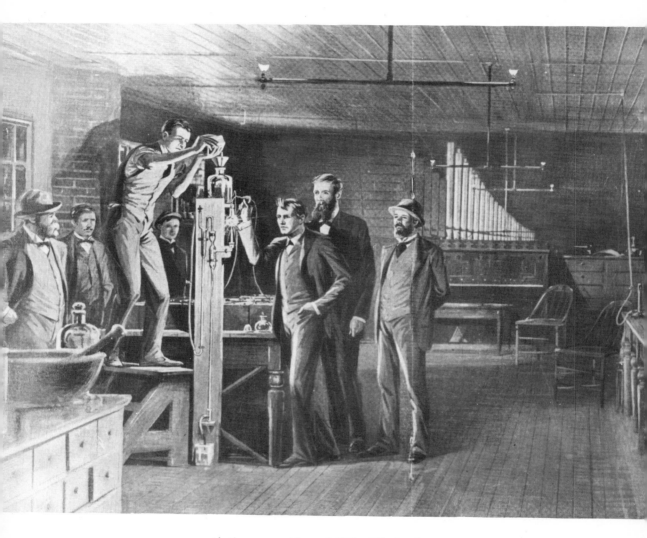

artist's conception of "The Birth of a Great Invention," showing Edison testing the first successful incandescent lamp at Menlo Park

Cities were once lit by gaslight.

ity today is carried in wires. In fact, gas is still used today to run stoves and furnaces in many homes. Gaslight, however, was flickery and funny-smelling. Edison felt that electricity would be a better way to light a home.

Edison was confident that he could invent an inexpensive and easy-to-use electric light where so many other inventors had failed. He even announced his plans publicly, to convince prosperous business people to lend him the money he needed for the project. But even Edison may not have guessed how difficult his search for the lightbulb was going to be.

He realized, as a few other inventors had, that the filament—the glowing strand—of an electric light needed to be sealed inside a glass container from which the air had been removed. This glass container was the "bulb" of the lightbulb. Air helped things to burn, and removing the air prevented things from burning. But even inside an airless bulb most filaments still fell apart within minutes.

He also needed a substance with high electrical resistance. Electrical resistance is the ability of certain substances to convert electricity into pure heat. It is this heat that would make the filament glow.

The search for the proper filament to put in a lightbulb inspired Edison's famous statement that "genius is 1 percent inspiration and 99 percent perspiration," which neatly sums up his approach to inventing. When an invention didn't work the first time—and few did—Edison simply rebuilt it in another way, until he found a way that worked.

In developing the lightbulb, Edison and his associates tried thousands of different materials before they found one that worked. The search went on for many months, and Edison must have despaired many times of finding a filament that would not burn up. He might, in fact, have given up the search, but he had put his reputation on the line by announcing in advance that he was going to invent a working lightbulb, and so he had to keep at it until he succeeded.

*The Edison Effect bulb was the forerunner of the vacuum
tube, which became the basis for modern communication—
wireless telegraphy, radio, and television.*

The search began in 1878. The first material that Edison seriously tested as a filament was platinum. It did not work. He tried other metals, and they didn't work either. His first success came using ordinary cotton thread. Before putting the thread in the bulb, however, he carbonized it—that is, he partially burned it, so that the actual filament was little more than a thread of ashes. As Edison later explained it:

> All night Batchelor, my assistant, worked beside me. The next day and the next night again, and at the end of that time we had produced one carbon out of an entire spool of . . . thread. Having made it, it was necessary to take it to the glassblower's house. With the utmost precaution, Batchelor took up the precious carbon, and I marched after him, as if guarding a mighty treasure. To our consternation, just as we reached the glassblower's bench the wretched carbon broke. We turned back to the main laboratory and set to work again. It was late in the afternoon before we had produced another carbon, which was again broken by a jeweler's screwdriver falling against it. But we turned back again, and before night the carbon was completed and inserted in the lamp. The bulb was exhausted of air and sealed, the current turned on, and the sight we had so long desired to see met our eyes.[10]

The bulb worked. A second bulb, made in the same manner, glowed for forty hours. As Edison said at the time, "If it can burn that number of hours, I know I can make it burn a hundred."[11]

This sketch, which appeared in a New York newspaper in 1880, shows Edison carbonizing filaments for his new electric light bulb.

But Edison did not abandon the search for filaments. Carbonized thread worked well, but Edison was a perfectionist. He instigated a search for the perfect filament, going so far as to send special agents around the world on a highly publicized quest for materials that could be used in lightbulbs.

———

The filament that Edison finally chose for his lightbulbs was, of all things, carbonized bamboo. However, this was not a result of his round-the-world search. One day Edison picked up a bamboo fan that someone had left on a table and wondered how it would work as a filament, a question that he probably asked of every substance that passed through his hands during that period.

In the last week of 1879, Edison put on a demonstration of the lightbulb at Menlo Park. He opened the laboratory to the public, so that everyone who was interested could see electrical illumination with their own eyes. And a lot of people were interested. According to the *New York Herald*, "For more than a week now [as of early January 1880] the entire establishment with its twenty or thirty skilled hands, has been practically at a standstill, owing to the throngs of visitors. They come from near and far, the towns for miles around sending them in vehicles of all kinds—farmers, mechanics, laborers, boys, girls, men and women—and the trains depositing their loads of bankers, brokers, capitalists, sightseers, hungry agents looking for business."[12]

Unfortunately, the visitors were frequently unruly. Fourteen of the lightbulbs were stolen and a vacuum pump that was used to

a replica of the first successful incandescent lamp, which burned forty hours and used carbonized cotton thread as a filament

[67]

create the bulbs was destroyed. But the demonstration served its purpose: the public was once again convinced that Thomas Edison could work miracles.

———

Even though he now had a working lightbulb, Edison's invention was not yet complete. The Wizard of Menlo Park understood something that other inventors searching after a working incandescent lamp had not. Not only was it necessary to find a way to make an inexpensive electric lamp, it was also necessary to find a way to supply the users of that lamp with the power that makes it work.

Nowadays, we take electricity for granted. We pay little attention to the networks of electric wires that carry electricity from power stations to houses, or the sockets on the wall into which we plug our electric appliances. For the most part, we don't notice these things until they fail and then we get angry at the electric power companies for not sending us the power we need to make our lightbulbs glow.

In Edison's time, however, there were no electric power companies, no electric wires carrying electricity to homes and offices, no sockets on the wall. If you needed electricity in the 1880s, you had to buy an electric generator, a luxury that only the rich could afford.

Edison did not intend for his lightbulb to be a toy of the rich. He wanted *everybody* to have electric lighting, and this meant finding a way to carry electric power from a central station into private homes, in the same way that gas was carried in pipes. Even as he announced his intention of inventing the incandescent lamp, this problem was in the front of Edison's mind. It was not enough to invent the lightbulb. He had to invent the electric power industry as well!

This meant that he had to find a way to send electric power over long wires without the power becoming weaker with dis-

the dynamo room at the Pearl Street Station

tance. He had to invent a method of powering many lightbulbs from a single wire so that if one lightbulb failed, the others would keep burning. He had to find a way of "subdividing the electric current" so that many bulbs could be powered by a single generator.

These were difficult problems, and there were many people, including highly respected scientists, who believed that they could never be solved. Edison proved them wrong. Even as he was working on the problem of finding the proper filament for his incandescent lamp, he was also working on the problem of distributing electric power to a whole network of lamps. To this end, he built a dynamo and a wiring system capable of generating electricity for hundreds of offices and homes. To demonstrate the system, he built a pilot plant in New York City: the Pearl Street Station. It was run by the Edison Electric Illuminating Company of New York, an ancestor of today's Consolidated Edison, known to New Yorkers as Con Ed. The Pearl Street Station supplied electricity for more than two hundred customers.

It was not an immediate financial success, however. At one point, Edison joked to his private secretary, Samuel Insull: "Sammy, do you think you can earn a living again as a stenographer? Because if you do, I think I can earn my living as a telegraph operator. So that we can be sure of having something to eat, anyway."[13]

CHAPTER SEVEN

Living Legend

If the invention of the phonograph had made Edison a national figure, the electric lightbulb turned him into a living legend. By the 1880s, Edison was one of the most famous men in the world.

In 1884, however, tragedy struck. Mary Edison, then only twenty-nine years old, caught typhoid fever. She was sick for several weeks, then suddenly took a turn for the worse. On August 9, 1884, she died. When Edison's daughter Marion awoke that morning, she "found him shaking with grief, weeping and sobbing so he could hardly tell me that mother had died in the night."

Edison was thirty-seven years old when his wife died. He was very much affected by her death. He pulled up stakes, moved away from the Menlo Park laboratory, and never came back, though the laboratory itself remained open for some years.

———

Edison plunged himself into the Pearl Street Project with considerable vigor, but he was lonely. He had three children to raise and

Mina Miller Edison

little time in which to raise them. His friends introduced him to a series of young women. Within six months of his wife's death he had met Mina Miller, who became his second wife.

With the new Mrs. Edison, the inventor moved his family into a brand-new home, a castlelike mansion in West Orange, New Jersey, called Glenmont. To go with his new home, Edison decided that it was time to build a new laboratory in West Orange, even larger than the one at Menlo Park.

Edison was now a man of the world. He traveled to Europe to demonstrate his inventions at large expositions and was entertained by heads of state. But he was still an inventor at heart and liked nothing better than to roll up his sleeves and work in the laboratory.

Now that he had solved the problem of the electric lightbulb, Edison turned his attention back to an invention that he had neglected for nearly ten years: the phonograph. What inspired him to pick up where he had left off was the discovery that other inventors were developing phonographs of their own and were going to market with them before Edison could go to market with his.

Two of these inventors, Chichester Bell (a cousin of Alexander Graham Bell) and Charles Sumner Tainter, approached Edison with an offer. They would do the work of developing an improved phonograph, but they wanted Edison's cooperation in the endeavor. As Edison's secretary later recalled the event:

They said that they fully recognized the fact that Mr. Edison was the real inventor of the "talking machine"; that their work was merely the projection and refinement of his ideas, and that they now wanted to place the whole matter in his hands and turn over their work to him without any public announcements that would indicate the creation of conflicting interests. They were prepared to bear the costs of all experimental work . . . and provide all the capital necessary for its

Top left: *Edison at Glenmont, his castlelike home in West Orange, New Jersey.* Bottom left: *the reception foyer at Glenmont. Edison entertained many dignitaries in his home in his later years.* Above: *this ivy-covered building houses the laboratory and library of Edison at West Orange, New Jersey.*

The library in the West Orange building.
It contains over 10,000 books,
Edison's desk, his cot (he reportedly
slept an average of only four hours a night,
often in the library), and many
works of art and other items of interest.

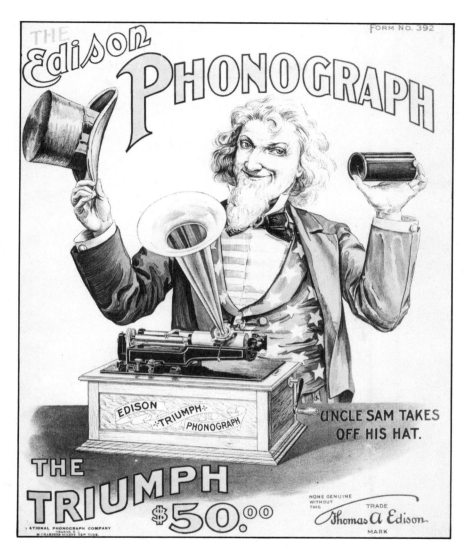

A poster for one of Edison's commercially developed phonographs. Note the wax recording in "Uncle Sam's" left hand.

exploitation. And for all this they asked to be accorded a one-half interest in the enterprise . . . Though they had tried to differentiate their instrument from his by calling it the Graphophone, if Mr. Edison would join them they would drop this name and revert to the original designation.[14]

The two inventors were probably quite surprised at Edison's reaction to this proposal. He called them pirates and declared that they wanted to steal an invention that was rightfully his. On no account would he cooperate with them, and he would fight them in the marketplace by building his own commercial phonograph.

Edison worked on the phonograph for the next two years, improving it in a number of ways. He replaced the tinfoil on the cylinder with wax, so that the cylinders could be used over and over again. He improved the needle so that it floated lightly over the surface of the wax. He even invented a method for duplicating the recordings, so that copies could be distributed for sale.

In 1888, he decided that it was time to put the machine on the market. To publicize his phonographs, he invited famous singers and musicians to his laboratory, to make recordings of their work.

Oddly, Edison downplayed the entertainment value of the phonograph. Perhaps he felt that mere personal amusement was too trivial a task for such an important machine. "I don't want the phonograph sold for amusement purposes," he said on one occasion. "It is not a toy. I want it sold for business purposes only."[15] Perhaps Edison saw the phonograph as a glorified dictaphone. Nonetheless, it was the entertainment value of the phonograph that was largely responsible for its popularity, especially the recording of music, which is what we are still using Edison's invention for today, more than a century later.

CHAPTER EIGHT

The Grand Old Man

In the following years, much of Edison's work concerned the inventions he had developed as a younger man. But while the younger Edison had an uncanny knack for pursuing an invention until he had found and perfected it, the older Edison sometimes found himself pursuing will o' the wisps.

One such will o' the wisp was direct current. Simply put, there are two kinds of electric current, direct current (DC) and alternating current (AC). All electricity is a flow of tiny particles called electrons. In direct current, the electrons flow in a single direction. In alternating current, the electrons rapidly alternate between two different directions of flow.

When Edison first developed his power stations, he used direct current, because this was the easiest type of current for the electrical technology of the 1880s to handle. In time, however, it became evident that alternating current was better for carrying electric power over long distances—evident to everyone except Thomas Edison.

Edison maintained for many years that alternating current was unsafe, even in the face of evidence to the contrary. This is not to say that Edison did not have reasons to take this position, based on his own research. But according to many historians his attitude in the argument bordered on the irrational. He apparently ignored evidence for the superiority of AC in favor of what evidence he could find for the superiority of DC. To prove his point, and to win points against his rival in the electric power business, George Westinghouse (a staunch supporter of alternating current), Edison resorted to some very dirty tricks. He performed cruel and widely publicized "experiments," electrocuting animals to show the dangers of alternating current. He even arranged for the nation's first electric chair, used to electrocute convicted murderers, to be powered by alternating current. Years later, Edison admitted that he had been on the wrong side in the "current wars," but not until alternating current had caught on despite his vigorous opposition.

———

Probably the best-known invention of Edison's later years was the motion picture, what we refer to today as the "movies." The motion picture was to the eye what the phonograph was to the ear, a method of recording moving images so that they could be played back again and again.

In the late nineteenth century, a number of inventors were working on ways of recording moving images. One of them was Edison and another was his young assistant, William Kennedy-Laurie Dickson. Edison and Dickson first developed a device that Edison called the "kinetoscope" in 1888. It was a cabinet containing a strip of film, with a sequence of pictures on it. A small hole in the side of the cabinet allowed a viewer to watch the film, one picture at a time. The sequence of pictures created an illusion of movement in the picture itself—hence the term "motion pictures."

Later, Edison added a slot to the cabinet into which the viewer

George Westinghouse (1846–1914)
asks his engineers to develop
an alternating current transformer key.

the kinetoscope

could drop a nickel to start the film moving, thus providing a way in which he could make money from the invention. He then set out to create a series of motion pictures that would make this 5¢ investment worthwhile. To this end, he constructed the world's first movie studio at the West Orange laboratory. Called the Black Maria, the studio was a 50-foot (15-m)-long wooden structure that could be turned on a giant pivot so that it always faced the sun, thus providing the illumination for the films. The first movies depicted prize fights, ballet dancers, famous people such as "Buffalo Bill," and just about anything else that struck the fancy of Edison's film crew.

Edison's role in the development of the kinetoscope has been a subject of considerable controversy in later years. Some historians give the most important role in the development of motion pictures to young Dickson, while others maintain that Edison was the driving force behind the invention. Whatever the case, for many years Edison's name was closely associated with motion pictures, though today we tend to remember him better for his role in the development of his earlier inventions, such as the incandescent lamp and the phonograph.

While the kinetoscope was under development, Edison was also working on one of his less successful inventions: the electromagnetic ore separator. This was a device that used a giant magnet to separate iron ore from sand. However, new supplies of cheap iron ore from the Midwest made the electromagnetic separator impractical, and Edison lost $2 million on the project. He didn't brood over the loss of the money. "Well," he said to an associate, "it's all gone, but we had a hell of a good time spending it!"[16]

———

Edison lived to a ripe old age, but he never lost his passion for work. During World War I, when he was in his sixties, he worked with the navy to find ways to protect American ships from Ger-

Black Maria, the world's first motion picture studio

man U-boats. In his later years, he was befriended by fellow inventor Henry Ford, who had developed the first affordable automobiles. Ford was much younger than Edison, but he worshipped the older man, and Edison in turn felt a great deal of affection for the younger inventor. They would vacation together in the country, pitching a tent and sleeping in the woods. These vacations became so well-known that the pair eventually had to stop because they were joined by too many members of the press. On one of their last jaunts, Edison and Ford were joined by no less eminent a person than Warren Harding, the president of the United States.

In 1929, Henry Ford became aware that the fiftieth anniversary of the invention of the lightbulb was drawing near. In honor of the aging Edison, he arranged to hold a special ceremony on the occasion. As part of the event, he rebuilt Edison's entire Menlo Park laboratory at the Ford factory in Dearborn, Michigan.

According to a reporter for the *Detroit Free Press*, Edison was quite moved when he saw the reconstruction. "As he walked to a chair and sat down, his companions in the party remained where they stood, apart from him a dozen feet. No word was spoken; it was as if by common consent the spectators instinctively felt awe here, in the presence of an old man upon whom the memories of eighty-two years were flooding back. He sat there, silent, his arms folded, an indescribably lonely figure, lonely in the loneliness of genius, of one who somehow had passed the others, who no longer has equals to share the world, his thoughts, his feelings.

"For five, perhaps ten, minutes, the scene was unmarred by a word or a gesture, except that now and then Edison looked about him and his eyes dimmed. Suddenly he cleared his throat and the spell was broken."[17]

When Edison saw the reconstruction that Ford had made of his laboratory from Menlo Park, he turned to the younger inventor and said that it was "ninety-nine and one half percent perfect!" Ever the perfectionist, Ford turned back to his mentor in

Henry Ford (1863–1947) with
one of his Model T automobiles

*Edison with Ford and President Harding
(right) on a camping trip*

some distress and asked, "What is the matter with the other one half percent?"

"Well, we never kept it as clean as this," Edison replied, perhaps with the hint of a sly grin on his face.[18]

The anniversary, which was attended by dignitaries as diverse as the Prince of Wales and the president of Germany, included a dinner at which Edison spoke. After speaking, however, Edison collapsed. It was to be his last public appearance.

His health never improved. In September 1931, Edison passed into a coma. He was eighty-four years old. On October 18, 1931, he died. It was proposed that lights across the United States be darkened briefly in the inventor's honor. For one minute, on the evening of October 21, this was done. Even the light on the Statue of Liberty was turned off.

After his death, his body lay in state for two days at the West Orange laboratory, where it could be viewed by the public. Among the thousands of people who visited the laboratory to pay tribute to the inventor were the president of the United States, Herbert Hoover, and his wife. Edison was then buried at nearby Roosevelt Cemetery, though he was later moved to the grounds of the Edison estate at Glenmont, next to the grave of his second wife, Mina.

————

During the course of his two marriages, Edison fathered six children, three—Marion, Tom, Jr., and Will—with his first wife, Mary, and three more—Charles, Theodore, and Madeleine—with Mina. He was never close to his children, but that was not uncommon in those days, when men worked long hours and women were expected to raise children largely on their own, or with the help of hired nursemaids.

None of the children followed in Edison's footsteps. Thomas Edison, Jr.'s, story is perhaps the most tragic. Unable to live up to the famous name he had been given, Tom, Jr., allowed himself to

*Edison (center, wearing cap) and his assistants
in the Menlo Park laboratory, which was
recreated by Henry Ford as part of
Greenfield Village in Dearborn, Michigan*

This memorial to Thomas Edison,
in Menlo Park, New Jersey, was
first lighted to mark the ninety-first
anniversary of the inventor's birth.
The huge bulb at the top uses 5,200 watts.

fall into the hands of unscrupulous businessmen who paid him money for the right to put the name Thomas Edison on their products. He suffered all his life from alcoholism and actually lived for a time, after the end of his first marriage, as a skid-row bum.

Marion, the eldest child, whom Edison had nicknamed Dot, believed that her father disliked her and moved to Europe to get away from him and her stepmother Mina, whom she disliked. She married a German army officer and settled in that country. Will, Edison's second son by Mary, was not very successful in later life, though he fared better than his brother Tom. For a time he ran an unsuccessful automobile dealership in Washington, D.C.; he eventually settled in Salisbury, Maryland, with his wife.

On the whole, Edison's children by his second marriage seemed to do better in life than their older siblings. Madeleine, who was reportedly quite intelligent and witty, married the son of a doctor. Charles, supposedly the personal favorite of Mina, was by one report "the only child [in the Edison family] who really got along with his father."[19]

Edison may have been the most famous man of his time. He was as well known as any movie star, perhaps better known even than the president of the United States.

He was one of the most remarkable men who ever lived. For a time, in the 1870s and 1880s, it seemed like Thomas Edison just might perform a miracle or two.

And perhaps he did. . . .

Footnotes

1. Matthew Josephson, *Edison: A Biography* (New York: McGraw Hill, 1959), 13.
2. Ibid, 14.
3. Ibid, 35–36.
4. Ibid, 44.
5. Robert Conot, *A Streak of Luck: The Life & Legend of Thomas Alva Edison* (New York: Seaview Books, 1979), 28.
6. Josephson, 74.
7. Ibid, 85.
8. Ibid, 163.
9. Ronald W. Clark, *Edison: The Man Who Made the Future* (New York: G.P. Putnam Sons, 1977), 79.
10. Ibid, 97.
11. Josephson, 220.
12. Clark, 99.
13. Clark, 141.
14. Josephson, 317–318.
15. Ibid, 326.
16. Ibid, 378.
17. Clark, 239.
18. Josephson, 479.
19. Conot, 403.

Recommended Reading

Clark, Ronald W. *Edison: The Man Who Made the Future.* New York: Putnam, 1977. Edison biography with emphasis on the development of his various inventions.

Conot, Robert. *A Streak of Luck: The Life & Legend of Thomas Alva Edison.* New York: Seaview, 1979. One of the most up-to-date biographies of the great inventor, with an emphasis on Edison the person rather than Edison the inventor.

Josephson, Matthew. *Edison: A Biography.* New York: McGraw Hill, 1959. A well-written biography of the inventor.

Silverberg, Robert. *Light for the World.* n.p. 1967. Edison biography with an emphasis on the development of the incandescent lamp and the power industry that would supply it with electricity.

Index

[94]